YOUR KNOWLEDGE HAS VALUE

AF141514

- We will publish your bachelor's and
  master's thesis, essays and papers

- Your own eBook and book -
  sold worldwide in all relevant shops

- Earn money with each sale

Upload your text at www.GRIN.com
and publish for free

Heidemarie Wawrzyn

The Hidden Album 1942 - 1943

Annotated Photo Presentation

GRIN Publishing

Bibliographic information published by the German National Library:

The German National Library lists this publication in the National Bibliography; detailed bibliographic data are available on the Internet at http://dnb.dnb.de .

This book is copyright material and must not be copied, reproduced, transferred, distributed, leased, licensed or publicly performed or used in any way except as specifically permitted in writing by the publishers, as allowed under the terms and conditions under which it was purchased or as strictly permitted by applicable copyright law. Any unauthorized distribution or use of this text may be a direct infringement of the author s and publisher s rights and those responsible may be liable in law accordingly.

Imprint:

Copyright © 2014 GRIN Verlag, Open Publishing GmbH
Print and binding: Books on Demand GmbH, Norderstedt Germany
ISBN: 978-3-656-58304-2

This book at GRIN:

http://www.grin.com/en/e-book/267976/the-hidden-album-1942-1943

GRIN - Your knowledge has value

Since its foundation in 1998, GRIN has specialized in publishing academic texts by students, college teachers and other academics as e-book and printed book. The website www.grin.com is an ideal platform for presenting term papers, final papers, scientific essays, dissertations and specialist books.

Visit us on the internet:

http://www.grin.com/

http://www.facebook.com/grincom

http://www.twitter.com/grin_com

Contents

Preface

Almost two years after the beginning of World War II, Nazi Germany invaded the Soviet Union in June 1941. SS mobile killing units followed directly on the heels of the *Wehrmacht*, the German army, and routinely rounded up Jews. With the assistance of the *Wehrmacht*, Jews were taken to extermination camps and killing fields.

Many German soldiers kept photo albums to recall their adventures and commemorate their "glorious days" in World War II. They had been in places where German killing units – *Einsatzgruppen* – had murdered Jews and anyone opposed to their advance. In towns like Grodno, Baranowicze, Bobruisk, Orel, and Briansk – hardly household names - Jews were sent to ghettos, forced into labor service, and routinely rounded up and massacred. The *Einsatzgruppen* and the German Army worked together. Logistical support including supplies, housing, and manpower were provided by the army. By spring 1943, over a million Jews and thousands of Soviet political commissars, partisans, and disabled persons were dead.

The starting point of the present project was the discovery of the hidden military album of my father who drove a truck through Belarus and Russia in 1942/43. The annotated photo presentation displays 24 black and white photographs. Dates and names of the depicted places were taken from the very few handwritten notes in the album; other dates had to be estimated on account of the absence of written documentation. Explanations of the pictures derive largely from the documentary "My Time of Service" (Richmond, VA 2005). Further details on towns, ghettos and killing sites were found in libraries and archives as well as on the Internet; those comments are written in italics.

For the most part the discovered photo album consists of ordinary pictures routinely taken during and after World War II – photos you can see in other military albums as well. But for one notable exception. That photo shows Jewish women, shovels in their hands, digging or closing graves. What is the background to that picture? What had happened there? How deeply was my father involved in the *Aktionen* against the Jews? In the presentation at hand, the author tries to find answers to these questions – questions which are difficult to solve almost seventy years after the Holocaust.

Acknowledgments

First of all, I want to thank the Virginia Holocaust Museum in Richmond/Virginia where Jay Ipson, the former director, and Charles Sydnor, the present museum head, advised and encouraged me to research my father's military album. My thanks also go to the former museum curator, Dianna Gabay who made it possible to digitize the photos in the album and store them on CD for future lectures and presentations. I also want to thank Tim Hensley, head of the museum's library and archives, for his help.

Last but not least, I want to express my thanks to the librarians and archivists of the Holocaust Memorial Museum in Washington, D.C. and Yad Vashem in Jerusalem for their warm assistance. My special thanks go to Donna Schatz who turned the discovery and contents of the album into a short documentary.

Jerusalem, 27 January 2014
Heidemarie Wawrzyn

The Hidden Album

1942-1943

(Annotated Photo Presentation)

Breaking the Silence

(Introduction)

When I was a child, Uncle George and his family often visited us on weekends in our small townhouse in Berlin which had been built during the Nazi era. My uncle loved to imitate Hitler and Goebbels and make fun of them. After his visit my parents used to say, "It's nice to have George here. But we don't like his mockery of Hitler and Goebbels." I did not ask why. When in 1979 almost the entire German nation watched the TV series *Holocaust*, my parents did not want to see it. I did not ask why. When my father mentioned the Second World War and added that he had driven a truck in Russia, I did not ask further questions.

Fig. 1: Near Livny (Orel, Russia) 1943.
Handwritten note "Vor dem Einsatz" (Before the action).

Then the day came when my father passed away. My mother's death followed eight years later. She was buried in the same cemetery where my grandmother and my father had been laid to rest. After the funeral I began to empty my parents' house. Among religious books, old music tapes and loose pictures, I found my father's military album stored in a cupboard in the living room. I hastily thumbed through its pages and decided to keep it for later study without knowing what I was going to discover there.

Many German soldiers kept photo albums to remember their wartime adventures. But I didn't know my father had done so too. All I knew was that he had driven a truck through Russia. When I looked through the album more carefully, I discovered he had been in places where German mobile killing units had murdered Jews, Communists, partisans and anyone opposed to the National Socialist regime.

My father received the album on his 23rd birthday in April 1940, probably the month he was drafted into the *Wehrmacht*. He sometimes labeled his photos. Some were dated. But many of them were just stuck into the album without a hint where or when they had been taken. There were pictures of him in Nazi uniform, as a *Wehrmacht* soldier, his comrade playing the accordion, clowning around with buddies on the grass. He drove his truck, repaired it, celebrated Christmas dinner in a bunker, and took pictures the same time that *Einsatzgruppen* were doing their murderous work in the East.

Looking closely at one snapshot, I could see a woman with a yellow badge on the back of her coat. In front there were women with shovels in their hands – on the back of the picture, the handwritten name of the town, "Baranowitsche" (Baranowicze). On the same album page, I discovered my father, cigarette in mouth, laughingly pulling a woman away from a truck in Brostowiza. These photos had never been shown to me. I was stunned, shocked, paralyzed.

I started researching the towns and locations displayed in the album. I searched the Internet and read books on the persecutions of Jews in Belarus and Russia. I went to Holocaust museums in Washington, DC, Richmond, VA and Yad Vashem in Jerusalem. I contacted the *Wehrmachts-*

Auskunftsstelle (Wehrmacht Information Center) in Berlin to get information on his military career. I wanted to know more about the Jewish communities in Belarus and Russia and my father's involvement in the Holocaust.

My father had been a soldier of the 383rd Infantry Division from 1942 to 1943. As a member of a supply unit, he drove "his" truck through Belarus and Russia from approximately March 1942 to August 1943. His division passed through locations where massacres of Jews and so-called partisans were frequently reported by the Security Police and the Security Service. His division had been in towns and sites where the subunits of the *Einsatzgruppe* B (SK 7b and EK 8)[1] had carried out actions.

In 2005, a friend of mine, an American documentarian, asked me for an interview about the album, its content, pictures and background. I agreed to be interviewed on camera which resulted in a short documentary on my father's military service during World War II. It simultaneously resulted in breaking his life-long silence about his Nazi past.

---

[1] *Sonderkommando* 7b (SK 7b) was active in Brest-Litovsk, Kobrin, Pruzhany, Slonim, Baranowicze, Minsk, Orsha, Klinzy, Briansk, Kursk, Tserigov, and Orel. It executed 6,788 people.

Einsatzkommando 8 (EK 8) was in Volkovisk, Baranowicze, Babruysk, Lahoysk, Mogilev, and Minsk. It executed 74,740 people
(http://en.wikipedia.org/wiki/Einsatzkommando).

His Time of Service

(Excerpts and Photos from a Documentary[2])

"IN JUNE 1941 WHEN GERMANY INVADED THE SOVIET UNION, FOUR LARGE KILLING UNITS – THE *EINSATZGRUPPEN* – FOLLOWED CLOSELY ON THE HEELS OF THE *WEHRMACHT*, THE GERMAN ARMY. THEIR TASK WAS TO ROUND UP AND ELIMINATE JEWS AND OTHERS DEEMED ENEMIES OF THE GERMAN PEOPLE. *EINSATZGRUPPE B* MOVED EAST FROM POLAND, THROUGH BELARUS AND CITIES SUCH AS GRODNO, BOBRUISK, BARANOWICZE, BRIANSK, AND OREL.

LOGISTICAL SUPPORT WAS OFTEN PROVIDED BY THE *WEHRMACHT*."[3]

Fig. 2: Father next to the truck.
The white 'J' stands for Supply Unit.

---

[2] Donna Schatz: My Time of Service, Richmond, VA, 2005.
[3] Ibid.

The only thing my father told me about World War II was that he had been in Russia. His job was to drive a truck and repair it whenever needed.

Fig. 3: In the West, probably in France, 1940.　　　*Fig. 4: Orel, Russia, June 1942.*

About his involvement in the Nazi party, he simply told me that he had joined the Hitler Youth (HJ). He liked being a member of the HJ program.

When I asked him why, he said it was because they allowed him to ride a motorbike. This was obviously his great passion.

The Motor-HJ was founded in 1933. The aim of the Motor-HJ was to create a pool of special forces and outstanding drivers for the Wehrmacht. To become a member of the Motor-HJ, you had to be at least 16 years old.[4]

Fig. 5: Vacations, Saxon Switzerland, 1939.

---

[4] Enzyklopädie des Nationalsozialismus, Munich, 1997.

Fig. 6: RAD Schönwalde [1939?]

Above you can see my father (far right) at the *Reichsarbeitsdienst* (RAD) in Schönwalde near the Baltic Sea. *From June 1935 men aged between 18 and 25 had to serve six months before they began their military service. During World War II the Reich Labor Service developed to an auxiliary formation which provided support for the Wehrmacht, the German Army.*

Fig. 7: On the beach. RAD, Schönwalde

Sometimes you see him and his comrades on a beach, having a picnic, and making music. This snapshot gives the impression that they had a lot of fun sitting on the beach and listening to the accordion. The scene gives not the slightest hint of war – nor that these men are soon going to the army.

All of a sudden the album shows pictures of the route to Russia through Belarus.

Fig. 8: To Kolpna (Russia)

Road conditions were very poor; everything was wet and muddy. You can see soldiers and at least one man with a white armband – building a road from wooden planks.

Fig. 9: Album page "On the way to Russia."

Handwritten note: ***"Near Lipowka"***

Fig. 10

Handwritten note: ***"Near Rungajew"***

Fig. 11

Fig. 12

The picture below is the crucial photo of the entire album because it clearly reveals a yellow badge on a woman's coat.

Fig. 13: Baranowicze, approx. 1942.

In the background, you can see a wooden building. In front there are women with shovels in their hands. They are digging graves or closing them. It is not clear if they were forced to dig graves for their own folk or for the bodies of dead German soldiers. But there is no doubt, this picture bears witness to Jewish forced labor. According to a handwritten note on the back of the photo, it was taken in Baranowicze, a town and an important railway junction in Belarus.

On July 31, 1942, a train from Theresienstadt arrived in Baranowicze; all the Jews had to leave the train and were killed on the spot in gas vans. Some Jews from the nearby camp in Koldyczewo were brought to close the victims' graves.[5] I wonder if this or a similar atrocity could be the background to the picture above.

Baranowicze was occupied by the German Army at the end of June, 1941. In June/July 1941, a killing unit of Einsatzgruppe B passed through Baranowicze on its way to Minsk. More than 400 Jews were murdered. Later, the Germans started establishing a ghetto in the southern part of the town and forced the Jews to live there from December 1941. Some 12,000 Jews were crammed into sixty barracks. From March to December 1942, three actions were carried out by the Germans and their collaborators. Many Jews were taken to nearby camps. Others were loaded onto trucks and transported from the ghetto to the killing sites. A few escaped to the forests. Only 250 of 12,000 Baranowicze Jews survived.[6]

---

[5] Yehuda Bauer, Jerusalem, 2003.
[6] Yehuda Bauer, Jerusalem, 2003.

Here is another very disturbing picture. The scene was shot in Brostowiza, another town in Belarus. A soup kitchen possibly provides food to local people. You see some local women standing at the open truck, around them soldiers laughing. Someone is pulling an older woman from the truck.

She seems to be holding or hugging another woman. And a soldier is pulling her away. I think that soldier is my father because he looks like him, a cigarette in his mouth.

This is not a situation where everybody is laughing. It is highly likely that the German soldiers alone were having fun.

Fig. 14: Brostowiza, 1942 [?].

A truck in Grodno, my father posing, his comrades posing as well. They look pretty relaxed despite the war.

The picture does not tell you that Grodno is unfortunately notorious for the actions of the *Einsatzgruppe* B.

The killing unit set out from Warsaw and moved east through Belorussia towards Smolensk. Thousands of Jews were deported from Grodno to various death camps in 1942/43.[7]

Fig. 15: Grodno, approx. 1942.

Local boys "reading" the Berliner Illustrierte Zeitung, a German news-paper. *This picture was probably taken for propaganda purposes.*

Fig. 16: Local boys reading a German newspaper
(date and location unknown).

---

[7] Samuel Spector (Ed.): The Encyclopedia of Jewish Life, New York, 2001; http://www.ushmm.org/wlc/en/article.php?ModuleId=10005130.

17

My father also took photos of local people, Russians, in front of their hut. Everything looks poor and muddy. On the back of the photo, he noted:

"So leben die Leute in Russland"
(That's how people live in Russia).

Fig. 17: Local Russians in front of a hut.

The following two images are apparently photos of the black market in Orel, Russia.

Fig. 18: Orel, 1942/43.   Fig. 19: Orel, 1942/43.

By December 1941, the majority of Jews had left Orel. The remaining Jewish families were transferred to a prisoner-of-war camp in Orel and housed in Block I. "On Wednesdays and Fridays, groups of six to eight prisoners were taken out to be shot. In 1942, the last group of Jews was taken to a forest where they were shot."[8]

Fig. 20: Christmas in a bunker, 1942.

Here you have a picture of Christmas. The year is written as 1942. Next to the photo you read, "Christmas in the bunker." You see my father, with the cigarette, sitting at a table with three of his comrades.

Next to this picture, he wrote,
"Before the retreat in 1943."

Fig. 21: Before the retreat in 1943.

Fig. 22: Probably during the retreat.

The war in Russia seemed to come to an end.

---

[8] Yitzhak Arad, 2009, page 199.

And then all of a sudden my father added vacation photos to the album: "Vacation 1944 at the Baltic Sea." You see my father on the beach while the war was still ongoing. I assume he got some time off from the war to recover from his travails.

Fig. 23: Baltic Sea, 1944.

On the one hand, the album contains pictures of soldiers and military vehicles and a few photos of Jews with their yellow badges. And then all of a sudden – the war not yet over – you get vacation snaps. Placing the holiday photographs admidst the wartime pictures, almost in the middle of the album, might well be an attempt to convey the message: Let's forget what happened. Let's get on with regular life.

Fig. 24: Dad, 1968.

As my father got older, he mentioned Hitler from time to time saying, "Actually, Hitler wasn't so bad except for the Jews." If I had the opportunity now to question him about World War II and the Holocaust, I would ask: "Do you know what happened there? Tell me more. And why didn't you say anything? Why didn't you tell your family about it?"

I hope he wasn't involved in murdering Jews. The photos prove, however, that he was in many towns and places where Hitler's mobile killing units were executing Jews. And Wehrmacht trucks were often used to transport Jews to the killing fields.

Maybe he did something to oppose the Nazi regime and its atrocities but I don't think so. I don't picture my father as a big hero, but rather as someone who wanted to get it behind him and continue his regular life. Once or twice, he said he had actually been lucky because he'd never had to shoot anyone. As a child, I always thought he was talking about a battle between Germans and Russians. But today I think he was talking about something else. Maybe he was referring to the execution of Jews, that he had never received the order to shoot ... Maybe.

End of documentary.

Appendix

HERE WAS A JEWISH CEMETERY
THIS GARDEN HAS BEEN DONATED
BY BARANOVICHI JEWS IN ISRAEL
AND THE WORLD TO THE MEMORY OF
12000 BARANOVICHI JEWS
KILLED BY THE NAZIS
AND THEIR COLLABORATORS
IN THE HOLOCAUST IN THE YEAR
1941 – 1944

The memorial plaque has been erected in the old Jewish cemetery of Baranowicze. During the war, mass murders were committed by a German killing squad at this site as well as in killing fields located in a forest on the outskirts of the city.[9]

---

[9] Eial Dujovny, 1999: To Baranovich
(http://www.jewishgen.org/belarus/newsletter/eial.htm).

Timeline:

Baranowicze, July 1941 – July 1942

"The Sonderkommandos (SK) and Einsatzkommandos (EK) reported on their extermination activities to their respective Einsatzgruppe headquarters which sent the information to Berlin. There the RSHA compiled concise reports ... The Einsatzgruppen Reports were discovered by the US Army in Gestapo headquarters in Berlin after the war."[10]

Excerpts: [11]

July 2, 1941:   EK 7b ... will proceed towards **Baranovichi** (Baranowicze, p. 3).

July 5, 1941:   EK 7b reports from Baranovichi systematic destruction of archives. Officials and clerks have fled. Church attendance is high (page 8).

July 24, 1941: Cooperation between the EK 8, based in **Baranovichi,** and the appropriate Army units is particularly successful. Together with the local military and civilian headquarters the formation of Jewish Councils, registration and concentration of Jews were brought about ... Actions were carried out continuously against Bolshevik agents, political commissars, etc. Another 301 persons were thus liquidated in **Baranovichi** (page 45).

---

[10] Yitzhak Arad et al. (Eds.): The Einsatzgruppen Reports. Selections from the Dispatches of the Nazi Death Squads' Campaign against the Jews, July 1941 – January 1943. New York, 1989.
[11] Ibid.

August 5, 1941:   Action against 157 Jews in **Baranovichi** (page 68).

August 5, 1941:   The unit of the *Einsatzkommando* 8 which is stationed in Baranovichi is particularly successful in its cooperation with the relevant units of the German Army. Together with the field and local commandants, they organized Jewish Councils, registration, and separate living quarters for Jews, as well as a new citizen registration ... (page 71).

August 12, 1941:   Executions were carried out in Minsk, **Baranovichi** ... (page 84).

March 2, 1942:   Increased partisan activity in the area of Slutsk and Baranovichi. ... A Jew was shot in public in the **Baranovichi Ghetto** because he refused to work (page 301).

March 9, 1942:   During an action against the Jews, carried out on March 2 and 3, 1942 Jews were executed in **Baranovichi** (page 307).

July 26, 1942:   Reports from the Occupied Eastern Territories, No. 9 ....

The Jews in Byelorussia: ... "The measures taken by the Security Police and the Security Service have created a fundamental change in Byelorussia as far as the Jewish question is concerned. Jewish Councils were set up in order to keep the Jews effectively under control, irrespective of the measures to be taken later on. These council were responsible for the behaviour of the members of their race. Moreover, Jews were registered and concentrated into ghetto. Finally, the Jews were identified with a yellow badge to be worn on the chest and on the back, like the Jew-star that has been introduced in the Reich. In order to make full use of the work potential of the Jews, they are generally used in groups for cleaning jobs. These measures have created the basis or the planned Final Solution of the European Jewish question specifically with respect in Byelorussia" (page 354).

Bibliography

Arad, Yitzhak: The Holocaust in the Soviet Union. Lincoln, 2009.

Arad, Yitzhak/ Krakowski, Shmuel/ Spector, Shmuel (Eds.): The Einsatzgruppen Reports. Selections from the Dispatches of the Nazi Death Squads' Campaign against the Jews, July 1941 – January 1943. New York, 1989.

Bauer, Yehuda: Jewish Baranowicze in the Holocaust, in Yad Vashem Studies 31, Jerusalem 2003, pp. 95-152.

Benz, Wolfgang/ Graml, Hermann/ Weiß, Hermann: Enzyklopädie des Nationalsozialismus. Munich, 1997.

Dujovny, Eial: To Baranovich and Back. Online Magazine, Issue No. 4/1999, (http://www.jewishgen.org/belarus/newsletter/eial.htm).

Headland, Ronald: Messages of Murder: A Study of the Reports of the Einsatzgruppen of the Security Police and the Security Service, 1941-1943, Fairleigh Dickinson University Press, 1992.

Longerich, Peter: Holocaust: The Nazi Persecution and Murder of the Jews, Oxford University Press, 2009.

Mallmann, Klaus-Michael; Cüppers, Martin: Crescent and Swastika: The Third Reich, the Arabs and Palestine. Ann Arbor: University of Michigan Press, 2006.

Rhodes, Richard: Masters of Death: The SS-Einsatzgruppen and the Invention of the Holocaust, New York, 2002.

Snyder, Louis L.: Encyclopedia of the Third Reich. New York, 1976.

Spector, Samuel (Ed.): The Encyclopedia of Jewish Life Before and During the Holocaust, New York, 2001.

Sydnor, Jr., Charles W.: Soldiers of Destruction: the SS Death's Head Division, 1933-1945. Princeton University Press, 1990.

Websites:

http://de.wikipedia.org/wiki/Einsatzgruppen_der_Sicherheitspolizei_und_d es_SD

http://en.wikipedia.org/wiki/Einsatzgruppen

http://kehilalinks.jewishgen.org/kholmich/theholocaust.htm

http://www.jewishgen.org/BELARUS/grodno1.htm

http://www.jewishgen.org/belarus/je_grodno.htm

http://www.jewishgen.org/belarus/newsletter/eial.htm

http://www.jewishgen.org/Yizkor/grodno/gro519.html

http://www.jewishvirtuallibrary.org/jsource/Holocaust/mobile.html

http://www.ushmm.org/outreach/en/article.php?ModuleId=10007710

http://www.ushmm.org/wlc/en/article.php?ModuleId=10005130

http://www.yadvashem.org/yv/en/holocaust/resource_center/item.asp?gate =2-30

US Holocaust Memorial Museum, Washington, DC:

RG-53.004 M	Grodno Oblast Archive records
RG-22.029	Selected records from the State Archives of the Orel Region
RG-14.068	Selected records of postwar ... court cases ... to Nazi war crimes

Yad Vashem Archives:

Einsatzgruppen Reports: O.53

Nazi Documentation, Wehrmacht: O.51

Personal Files of SS members from the Berlin Document Center: O.68

Records of Bundesarchiv Freiburg, Duplicates at YV: M.29.FR

Records of Extraordinary State Commission to Investigate German-Fascist
Crimes: M.33

Records of the Nuremberg Military Tribunal, Interrogation Reports: TR.2

Records, Archives in Belarus; duplicates at YV: M.41

Reports of Sich.Div. 221

Testimonies: M.1.E, O.3, M.10.AR.1

Trial Documentation: O.4

Wehrmachts-Auskunftsstelle

Wehrmacht Information Center in Berlin.

Documentary

Schatz, Donna: My Time of Service, Richmond, VA, 2005.

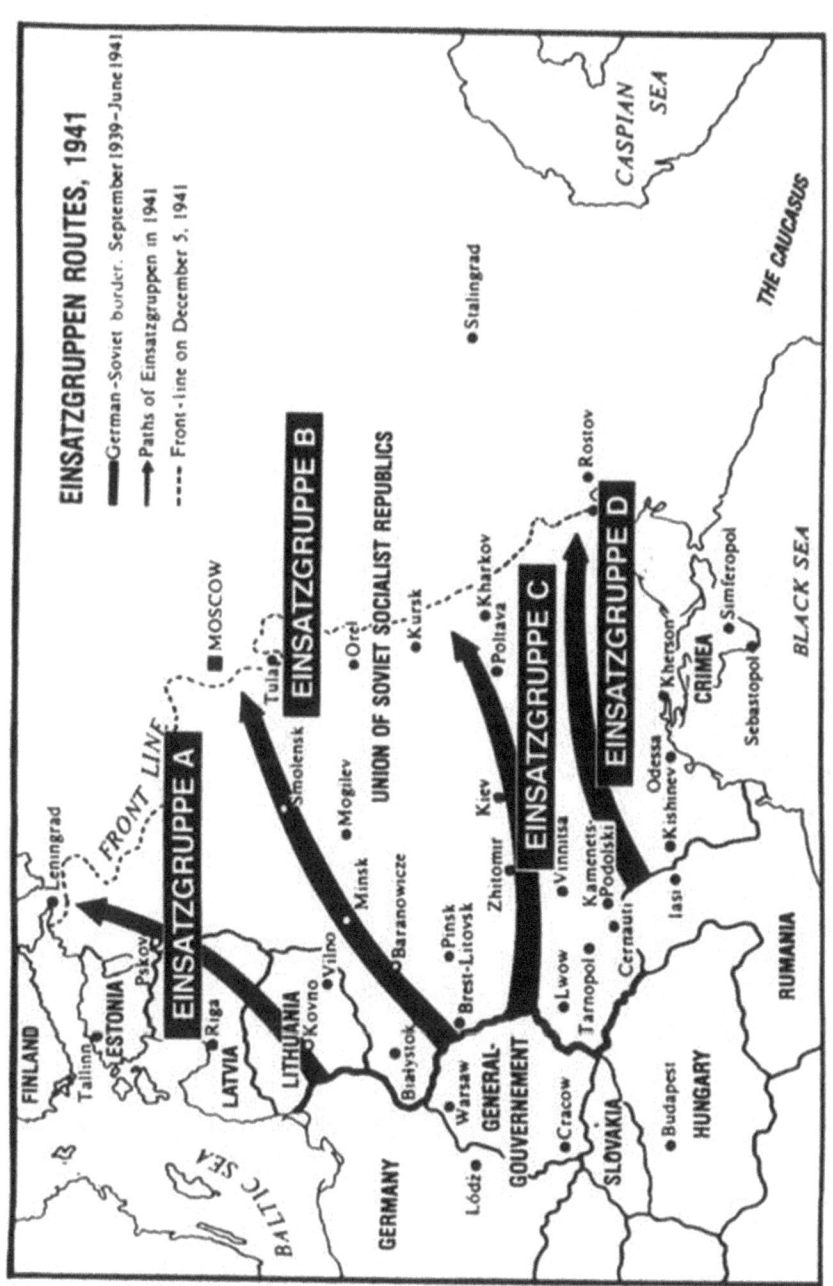

(Source: http://kehilalinks.jewishgen.org/kholmich/theholocaust.htm)